Rhyming Fun

Edited By Debbie Killingworth

First published in Great Britain in 2020 by:

Young Writers
Remus House
Coltsfoot Drive
Peterborough
PE2 9BF
Telephone: 01733 890066
Website: www.youngwriters.co.uk

Book Design by Ashley Janson

Softback ISBN 978-1-83928-984-2

Printed and bound in the UK by BookPrintingUK
Website: www.bookprintinguk.com
YB0445Z

FOREWORD

Here at Young Writers our defining aim is to promote the joys of reading and writing to children and young adults and we are committed to nurturing the creative talents of the next generation. By allowing them to see their own work in print we believe their confidence and love of creative writing will grow.

Out Of This World is our latest fantastic competition, specifically designed to encourage the writing skills of primary school children through the medium of poetry. From the high quality of entries received, it is clear that it really captured the imagination of all involved.

We are proud to present the resulting collection of poems that we are sure will amuse and inspire.

An absorbing insight into the imagination and thoughts of the young, we hope you will agree that this fantastic anthology is one to delight the whole family again and again.

CONTENTS

THE POEMS

Moving Transport

Cars
Cool, charming
Fast, driving, travelling
Steamy, smoking transport, super-fast deep space explorer
Four wheels, one engine
Steamy, smoking, super fast
Hot, fiery
Rocket.

Joshua Evans (8)
Bracken Hill School, Kirkby In Ashfield

Really Cool!

Running
Fast, speedy
Racing, winning, smiling
Free like a bird, fresh air and exercise
Good times, fun, happiness
Cool, really awesome
Games.

Connor Parkin (8)
Bracken Hill School, Kirkby In Ashfield

Pizza Monster

Pizza
Big, scary
Breaking buildings
Blasting cheese
Changing people into pizza
Crunching bones, toxic
Bringing aeroplanes down
Scary.

Jordan Knight (10)
Bracken Hill School, Kirkby In Ashfield

Destroying And Winning

Hero
Warrior man
Fighting, defending, winning
Throw him in the trash, shutting down
Destroying, exploding, kicking
Evil, scary
Robot.

Oliver Morley-Blunt (10)
Bracken Hill School, Kirkby In Ashfield

Films

Film
Funny, scary
Laughing, smiling, frightening
Black and whites, sitting and watching
Children, family
Shops, stores
DVD.

Charlie Morgan (10)
Bracken Hill School, Kirkby In Ashfield

Eight Spheres And A Star

We are the planets of the solar system
Different sizes for everyone
Some are rock and some are gas
And we all orbit the sun.

We call the sun, singing first on this track
I'm the centre of the solar system, planets all around
I'm so hot, boiling, burning all year round.

I'm Mercury, the smallest planet, smaller than the moon
I get super hot and super cold and spin too slow

I'm Venus, I've got volcanoes that spray
I'm the same size as Earth but spin the opposite way

Hey, this is the Earth, a home to everyone
I'm such a beautiful little world

Look, I'm Mars, I've got deserts and ice
I've got two moons, like one moon but twice

I'm Jupiter, the biggest planet, I'm humongous and gigantic
I spin the fastest, sing the loudest and the most majestic

Oh, hi! I'm Saturn, look at my beautiful rings
Made up of billions of rocks, matter and other things

I'm Uranus, I say that with pride. Okay, I lied
'Cause I'm embarrassed as I lie on my side

I'm Neptune, cold, dark and mysterious
I'm very stormy, bring an umbrella, I'm serious

This is our solar system
Take care of it
This is the end of the poem
Thanks for reading it.

Shiven Agarwal (11)
Holyport CE (A) Primary School, Holyport

The Solar System

I want to fly to space
Earth will be my base
I will visit planets eight
My rocketship operates
I want to feel the different atmospheres
Like all the astronauts for many years
I'm going to travel higher
Until I reach the sun's hot fire
Onto Mercury, this planet is so small
All the rocks and metal, I must be careful not to fall
A quick break at Venus for completeness
It has no water and is very hot
So best not to stop
Next onto Mars
There are no cars
Rocky red mountains to climb
But oh no, we have no time
Jupiter is spinning so fast
How will I ever last?
This is the biggest ball of gas

I hope my rocket doesn't crash
Landing on Saturn will need to be concise
As it is surrounded with rings of ice
Stopping at Uranus is a must
But how will I land with all those rings made of dust?
Neptune, with its cold, wet storm
Makes me want to go home to the warm
I enjoyed my trip into space
But I'm glad to be back at base
Earth is the home I love.

Willcox (10)
Holyport CE (A) Primary School, Holyport

The Lost Astronaut

I'm floating in a void of darkness
Lost without a hope of ever going back
To my old home on Earth
Because I'm stuck in nothing but black.

My rocket was blown into bits
My mouth won't scream, I can't make a sound
And I will never ever ever again
Be able to touch the ground.

And all of this because of my job
It seems quite silly really
On the rocket I bashed my head
So I couldn't control clearly.

Then an asteroid hit the rocket
Flames went up in every place
I didn't do anything to stop it
So now it's just me lost in space.

To be honest I barely made it out alive
Because the others took the escape pod

I think they left me to perish
As my friend gave me the death nod.

If you find this little note
Please come and try to save me
It's not very fun up here
And I'm getting extremely lonely.

Lucy Gay (11)
Holyport CE (A) Primary School, Holyport

Solar Souls

"I'm feeling so blue, no one ever visits me and I have nothing to do," cried Neptune.

"My moons all mock me. I'm ever so grand, but they remain faithful, my satellite band," said Jupiter.

"I love to dance and sing, but most of all to show off each colourful ring," Saturn boasted.

"I'm very quick this close to the sun, but everyone knows I'm the hot one!" glowed Mercury.

"I'm terribly shy; I don't like a crowd. I keep my love safe 'neath my wispy, cream cloud," giggled Venus.

"I'm really far out, not easily seen. I'm really laid back with a serious lean," shivered Uranus.

"Marching along, trailing red dust, the other planets think I'm covered in rust," Mars barked.

"I'm the cradle of life, spinning alone, proud of my place in the Goldilocks zone," Earth smiled.

Gloria Smith (10)
Holyport CE (A) Primary School, Holyport

Wonders Of Space

If it were possible I would give to you
The wonders of space too good to be true
Eight round planets like Saturn and Mars
Trillions and billions of twinkling stars
When you look at the light it's really the past
Though light still travels really fast.

If it were possible I would give to you
The wonders of space too good to be true
Saturn's rings, what a sight
Showing off in all their might
Pluto is classed as a dwarf planet
It's still with the rest, under a night sky blanket.

If it were possible I would give to you
The wonder of space too good to be true
Asteroid belts that are still in their place
Whilst comets are busy whizzing through space
Millions of facts have all been found
But many more are still around.

Jessica Hancock (10)
Holyport CE (A) Primary School, Holyport

Planetary Poem

First is Mercury, the hottest of the hot
I promise if you touched it it would burn a lot
Next up is Venus which spins different from the others
This took a while just to discover
Here comes Earth, the only one with life
Which is why we grow plants just to survive
Mars is the fourth planet from the sun
If you had a ton the gas would be done
Jupiter, the biggest of them all
It has a great red spot that creates a big storm
We are getting to the route, now we have Saturn
Its beautiful wings create a whimsical pattern
Next is Uranus, always made fun of
Now Uranus is angry, he's had enough!
Last is Neptune, I don't have a rhyme
So I will skip it and not waste your time!

Soha Alam (10)
Holyport CE (A) Primary School, Holyport

A Journey Through Space!

Go out past this world, speed into the sky.
Zoom past the stars, to planets you'll fly!

Look into space, see stars oh so bright.
They're blinding the sky, oh what a sight!

See Saturn's rings? How amazing they are!
No one has been there, for it is too far.

Look over there! Millions of miles from the sun,
That looks like Mars. Oh how this is fun!

See that black hole? Don't go too near.
For the force is too strong, and you will have fear!

Astronomers are bright, astronomers are cool!
Don't underestimate them, for you'll be a fool!

Sasha White (11)
Holyport CE (A) Primary School, Holyport

Alone And Lost In Space

Floating through the nothingness
Alone and lost in space
An empty void stretches before me
Stars scattered across its face.

I miss the ones I love back home
Alone and lost in space
All my friends and family
When will I get out of this place?

I'm isolated and miserable
Alone and lost in space
Right now in this moment
I long for a warm embrace.

I notice a shooting star
Alone and lost in space
Wait, no, that's a rocket
To take me back to base.

Reunited with my family
No longer lost in space

Returned from my long voyage
Back among the human race.

Carys Edwards (10)
Holyport CE (A) Primary School, Holyport

The Space Race

Astronauts or cosmonauts
Both countries had the thirst
To conquer the moon-landing
Whose feet would land there first?

Russia's raging rocket ready 1961
Blasted Yuri to the atmosphere
The space race had begun
But Yuri didn't reach the moon
His mission was instead to orbit the Earth's stratosphere and put
Russia ahead.

America acted quickly and in 1969
Apollo 11 blasted off with history to redefine
When Armstrong's foot touched the moon the words that he could find were:
"It's a small step for man,
One giant leap for mankind."

Oliver Hanlon (11)
Holyport CE (A) Primary School, Holyport

The Space Planets

It's very cold and dark in space
In fact, it's a very big place
The sun is on fire and hot
Some people say you can live there but I say you cannot!
Mars is red and very cold
It's been around a long time, it's very old
There's a planet called Saturn that has many rings
If you wanted to get there you would need really strong wings
Jupiter is the biggest of them all
It has a big spot that looks like a big red ball
That's just a few of the planets in space
As you can see it's a very interesting place.

Lucas Richardson (10)
Holyport CE (A) Primary School, Holyport

Space

Space: an anonymous entity,
Space: from glistening light beams to mysterious black holes,
Space: great wisps of starlight hanging onto the unchartered abyss,
Space: sparkling stars scorching through the neon night light,
Space: UFOs, objects flying, undetected and unidentified,
Space: asteroid belts carrying millions of years of history,
Space: sleeping satellites drifting gracefully,
Space: a frenzy of multicoloured planets, life undetermined,
Space: an infinite cosmic opportunity yet to be discovered.

Zachary Cowan (10)
Holyport CE (A) Primary School, Holyport

Sailing Out To Space

I dream of going out to space,
Upon a yacht of stars,
To and from the Milky Way,
I would stop, amazed, and gaze at Mars.

With stars in front and stars behind,
And planets far and near,
I would ride upon Saturn's rings,
And search the whole stratosphere!

Now I'm on my way back home,
I'm flying around all alone,
My adventure ends here now,
But I will find my way back, somehow.

Aubrey Vorster-Davids (11)
Holyport CE (A) Primary School, Holyport

Snowy Town

The snowy town is a peaceful snowy town.
That is why couples go there, to have peace.
It is snowy.
And there are blossom trees that grow fast.
And children like to ride their new bikes and scooters.
There are lots of rich people who live there.
People walk there almost every day.
People say that it is so peaceful that Adele once lived there.
That is why people have good luck finding Adele in that place.
Only if they live there of course.
Over two hundred people live there.
It is so quiet, peaceful and a great busy town.

Gina Currie (8)
Jenner Park Primary School, Barry

Chess

Chess game started
Sitting, persuing the situation
Planning pawns' position
Bright knight taking pieces
Patiently fearing my opponent
The conquering king invades the squares
Blessed bishop moving diagonally
Mission getting pieces
Sneaky queen doing what it wants
Getting the king in checkmate
Feeling emotional and relieved
Because I won, yes!

Iestyn Jones (10)
Jenner Park Primary School, Barry

The Arctic Wolf

A n animal so cute
R aised in the snow
C old, cute, cunning
T eaching its cub to survive
I nvincible, incredible ice
C areful, curious comrades

W andering wolves walking in the snow
O bstacles intervening in their lives
L uxurious, lovely, loving
F antastic, fearless friends...

Dale O'Meara (11)
Jenner Park Primary School, Barry

Max

Max is a cute chihuahua
He's adorable
He is soft and fluffy
He's small and a tiny chihuahua
Max is a lovely chihuahua
Is a chatty puppy
Adorable as he can be
He can be messy and crazy
Delightful chihuahua
He is cute and small.

Kayden William Sansome
Jenner Park Primary School, Barry

Our Earth Is Dying

P lastic is killing the Earth
L ives at risk
A nimals dying
S ad turtles crying
T ime is running out
I t's time to make a change
C ome on, guys, our world is strange.

Charlie Bullen (10)
Jenner Park Primary School, Barry

Hot Chocolate

I love hot chocolate
I love to drink it
It's amazing to me
It's delicious
It's chocolatey goodness
It hydrates me
It's very very hot
Hot chocolate is my life!

Zac Bennett (8)
Jenner Park Primary School, Barry

Max

Max is cute
Max is lovely
Max is fluffy
Max is funny
Max is cuddly
Max is cheeky
Max is beautiful.

Alfie Bullen (8)
Jenner Park Primary School, Barry

What If You Lived In Space?

Have you ever wondered about living in space?
Wouldn't it be such an imaginary place?
What if you met galactic creatures,
Imagine all of their different features.
You could meet smart aliens,
Maybe they're Uranian.
Or aliens a bit stupider,
Maybe they're from Jupiter?
But on Mars
There'll be lots of stars.
Then you'll find Mercury why so small,
It's just like a tiny little ball,
And if you look at Saturn,
You'll see a beautiful pattern.
That's it for space,
Such a magical place!

Jaidan Mapara (9)
Langmoor Primary School, Oadby

The Glamorous Glowing Galaxy

First, let's start off with big bold red Mars
Or let's start off with the planet that has bars.
In space there are no cars but don't feel blue
Because there's something even better -
The bright glowing stars.
Now let's talk about the galaxy's sky,
It's so pretty it will make you burst into tears and cry.
Also, the best thing you could know
Is space because it lights up and glows.
Space is as shiny as a diamond ring,
When you look at the stars
They will blind your eyes and go bling.
It's time to go away from space
And when you're home you will feel out of place
But if you go to the galaxy
Please tell me what you see
Because all I know is the stars will always glow!

Delilah Smith (8)
Pluckley CE Primary School, Pluckley

Bluey The Monster

It was mid-winter and very, very cold,
I am Bluey the monster,
I am fluffy, furry and nice to hug.
I am also nice, caring and don't forget gentle.
The other people kicked me out of my home
So I looked high, low, side to side,
For a lovely home that people wouldn't kick me out of.
"Maybe you can help me," said Bluey.
"Yes," the girl replied.
"Yes, I have always wanted a pet monster like you.
You will always be loved."

Millie Archer (7)
Pluckley CE Primary School, Pluckley

Bob

Bob was a planet that was fiery and blue.
He was the only planet that flew,
He had bright green eyes,
And he was very wise,
And he loved the taste of home-made stew.

Bob likes to look at the shiny yellow sun,
While having lots and lots of fun.
Bob lives in space,
Where the stars race.
When Bob is hungry he has a bun.

Florence Fryd (7)
Pluckley CE Primary School, Pluckley

The Boy Who Dreamed Of Going To Space

A boy planned to go to space,
So he started to build a rocket base.
He built his rocket with iron and steel,
But he just didn't have the skill,
To blast his rocket way up high,
Miles and miles into the sky.
So today his dream crashed to the ground,
But tomorrow his dream will again be space-bound.

Dominic Glasgow (8)
Pluckley CE Primary School, Pluckley

On The Moon

There were some aliens,
They lived on the moon,
They were beautiful and slimy
And they hummed a tune.

The children gazed out of the window,
They wondered, *is it true*
That tiny, slimy creatures
Are as real as me and you?

Lily Jacqueline Humphreys (8)
Pluckley CE Primary School, Pluckley

I Love Space

I really like space, it is beautiful and the stars are as bright as the blazing hot sun

L ike space it will fill your imagination with joy!
O f all the planets my favourite one is Saturn, I love the ring around it
V enus is really close to the bright and pretty sun
E arth is magical, it's one of the best planets in the magnificent world

S aturn is magnificent with its bright ring around it
P erfect planet is Jupiter, the colours are amazing
A mazing planets they all are
C elebrate space, it is part of the amazing world
E xcellent space, it is the best part of the world.

Harriet Turner (8)
Quainton CE Combined School, Quainton

My Dogs!

My dogs are cute and sweet
Even though they chew my feet
They play, they fight
and they only rest at night.

They eat raw meat
and dance to the beat.
And they get so messy when they get back from their walk
Oh how I wish they could talk!

I always want to dress them up in what I wear
Apparently if dogs are scared, they may bite,
or perhaps if they get in a fight!

Some dogs like to catch a ball,
my dog doesn't, so not all!

My dogs are very noisy
especially when they play with their toysies!
They love chasing birds on the field,
and they have fur like a shield.

Ellie Whitlock (9)
Quainton CE Combined School, Quainton

It Needs To Stop

We're killing the Earth and that's just not fun
No one believes us because we are young
The trees are turning into flames in a second
And animals are dying in the sea, that's depressing
So get up and start helping the world get back to its good old self
We're spending too much time in our cars and that's a fact
Get out and walk a mile, it's not that hard.

So just you and me can do something small
To get our sea nice and clean
I am doing my best so can you
People act like the sea is a bin, it's a sin
We are all monsters if we keep doing this
So you know it needs to stop.

Ava Pacetti (8)
Quainton CE Combined School, Quainton

Monsters Meet Monsters

There are two monsters as tall as mountains
They are as frightening as a tiger, crushing everything they see
Two enemies bigger than Big Ben
Hearts full of hate
Faces full of anger
Terrifying monsters walking the planet
Loads of blood on their giant hands
Godzilla and murderous King Kong!
They're both so snappy and hurtful and hard
They fight and then get a massive fright
By a new monster which has awakened
They work, they shoot with no fear
And can't get defeated
They still live today in a horrible way.
Aargh!
Oh no!

Charlie Spriggs (9)
Quainton CE Combined School, Quainton

The Dumb Outlaw

He is a dumb outlaw
He steals for sure
Instead of a horse, he rides a tricycle
Which he thinks is cool!

He eats raw meat
And dances to the wrong beat
He shoots his gun to his team
And thinks he's a great guy.

He says haw-yee
Instead of yee-haw
He doesn't pay fees
And steals cheese
In the wild west!

He has a tiny brain
And he likes to eat the rain
He is funny
His friends are dummies
In the wild west!

Charlie Richardson (9)
Quainton CE Combined School, Quainton

My Favourite Things, Friends

She's funny,
She's small,
And she likes to be cool,
She's mad,
She has a dad,
And her brother smells bad.

Her sister runs down the street,
And likes to eat sweets,
She runs into the house
And then sees a mouse.

Her sister starts screaming,
When the bells are ringing,
When she's singing,
Her sister goes swimming.

Rita is my best friend,
Because she's funny,
She's silly, she's crazy

A little bit and she's like
Someone special to me.

VieVie Jo Harris (9)
Quainton CE Combined School, Quainton

I Like Trains

I like trains,
Although they can be a pain.
My favourite is steam,
They have a bright beam.
Sometimes they go *crash!*
And end up in the trash.

Electric is cool,
Although they don't have pools.
They're as modern as the Aston Martin DB11.

Finally, dumb, dirty diesels who aren't that good now,
Some engines go *pow*,
They're as slow as a cow.

I like trains, *yeah!*

Oliver Beesley (9)
Quainton CE Combined School, Quainton

I Want A Puppy

I want a puppy
Tell me please, when will I get it?
Please, please, please.
I want a puppy
Tell me when you can
Because you know I'm not a rich man.
I want a puppy
So don't get me mad
So please, go get my old dear dad.
I want a puppy
A little cute one
But they always chew your boot.
I want a puppy
The cutest can be
To say to the world
Now I've got a puppy!

Cherice Julianna Greff (9)
Quainton CE Combined School, Quainton

Universal

She was swept off her feet
By a man whose skin was as orange as a tangerine
He sailed the universe and into
A black hole as dark as charcoal.

The ship's hull rose with steam and
They smashed into a mountain of yellow
He opened the doors and she leapt
Onto a patch of sugar.

It felt as soft as snow
She rose to her feet and saw a
Horizon of milk and butter.

Ben Cane (11)
Quainton CE Combined School, Quainton

Journey Through The Night

A nd it's based in the forest
D rive a bus away in the woods
V ehicles help you and save you
E nd of the world
N ext to some dinosaurs
T hey walk trembling
U ndercover in bushes
R escue everybody and everything
E nd of the bend of the River Thames.

Frazer York (8)
Quainton CE Combined School, Quainton

The Awakening Nightmare

As I turn
I head to the stairs
Where I hear
Bang, bang, bang.

So I turn the handle
Who is there? A man in black
Holding a sharp blade
Still asleep I hear,
"Come here..."

Leah Gibson (11)
Quainton CE Combined School, Quainton

Galaxies

A lone, massive, pale white dot way up in the sky,
I sit outside and gaze at you as I get so high.
I think of things, I speculate beyond our atmosphere,
But sadly I'm no astronaut so I'm firmly planted here.
I think of meteors, I think of galaxies and thoughts we just cannot comprehend,
And petrifying things like black holes and exploding stars that could cause this world to end.
I glance back at the moon, it looks so beautiful, so radiant and yet so bizarre,
Amazing to think a mere human on Planet Earth really could travel so far.
Questions float up in my head like how far we could go and what resources are to gain?
And how far could someone stay up in space without going completely insane?And so I slip back to reality with thoughts still fresh in my head,
As I walk and take a glance, a peek before I lie drowsily on my bed.

Esther Godwin (9)
Queen Boudica Primary School, Colchester

Solar System

Our solar system is immense,
Planets with atmospheres that are dense,
But not for Mercury,
It has no atmosphere you can see.
But for Venus, it is the opposite,
Venus is the densest terrestrial, so it is the nominate.
Earth is Venus' sister,
That can glister.
Mars is almost in the Goldilocks zone,
But on the surface, there isn't even a bone.
Next is the colossal Jupiter,
With raging thunder.
Saturn's rings are extensive,
But they're slowly disappearing and those are the consequences.
Uranus is very unique
But is very bleak.
Next is Neptune, which is linked with my zodiac sign,
And, in my opinion, divine.

Ethan Atanacio (10)
Queen Boudica Primary School, Colchester

Sensational Space

S upernatural.
E xtra-galactic, outside the Milky Way.
N eptune, the eighth planet from the sun.
S aturn, the second-largest planet.
A stronauts and asteroids.
T errestrial planets (Mercury, Venus, Earth, Mars)
I ntriguing, like shooting stars.
O rbital period - some short, some long.
N eutron star, a collapsed and dense star.
A xis is a line which a planet rotates.
L imitless.

S un and the stars.
P lanets (Mercury, Venus, Earth, Mars, Jupiter,
Saturn, Uranus, Neptune).
A n absolute magnitude.
C omets.
E arth, our home planet.

Ava Wingate (9)
Queen Boudica Primary School, Colchester

The Galaxy I Most Adore

So many things beyond space,
I wish I could explore,
Every planet has its own beauty,
Mars, Uranus, Neptune?
Much more,
But one thing I really want to venture,
Is the thing I want to set myself free on,
The galaxy I most adore,
Our galaxy is the Milky Way,
Which glistens like diamonds j'adore,
Its colours are unicorns which are set free in space,
Galloping, zooming, flying,
Sprinkling pearl-coloured dust in the distance.
The galaxy's opaque colours make me want to
float into outer space,
Exploring, searching, examining,
Finding curious, fascinating objects to observe,
In the galaxy I most adore.

Varsha Basavaraja (10)
Queen Boudica Primary School, Colchester

My Haru

When I saw you, you were so small,
You mean the world to me, my little furball.
From the first moment I loved you so,
With your adorable paws running across my bed very slow.

Those teeny-weeny ears can listen to me for years,
Sometimes it's better to spend time with you than my own peers.
When I look into your glittering eyes, they look so wise,
That's why you are making all that mess before sunrise.

You are as precious as a diamond to me,
Because you are always jumping around with glee.

I adore you Haru, as much as I love lemon ice tea.

Amy Nguyen (10)
Queen Boudica Primary School, Colchester

Monkeys That Went To Mars

On a tree far away sat a small brown monkey,
He was staring at the night sky dreaming of Mars.
"Mars, Mars, I wish I could go to Mars.
It's so red," he said.
"It must be made of hot chilli sauce.
Yum-yum I love chillis,
I'm off to Mars," he said.
He knew of an old broken rocket in the jungle,
He quickly fixed it with some banana skins,
Palm leaves and sticky tape.
He fuelled the rocket with some leftover
strawberry jam.
"Mars here we come!" he said
As he took off in a loud explosive squelch!
Kaboom!

Austin Mason (10)
Queen Boudica Primary School, Colchester

Werewolf

With the curse bestowed on his heart,
The blood drenched the previously milky-white moon.
He transformed into a hideous beast with a glimmering coat of shadow.
His toes had razor-pointed tips
From the power of the blood-coated moon.
He had poison claws and teeth,
He considered his next victim and then he raced like a dart.
Then he heard a cartoon, he would get a meal soon.
He cheeped to the man
And leapt with a blood-curdling growl,
But the man held out a towel.
"Do not hurt me,
I will look after you and your doggy day form."

Conor Leonard (10)
Queen Boudica Primary School, Colchester

The Wonder Of Books

From books about space to books about the seas,
Books about animals and books about trees.
Books about wizards and The Hunger Games,
Chocolate and Charlie, Peaches and James.
The Baddest Dad and an Awful Auntie,
Gerald a giraffe who is quite prancy.
Railway Children and a Highway Rat,
A Gruffalo and Tabby McTat.
Dragons and Bear Hunts, you'll find in the gloom,
Where's Gangsta Granny? Is there Room on the Broom?
From books written by experts to ones written by cooks,
Escape to the pages, this is the wonder of books.

Emily Newton (10)
Queen Boudica Primary School, Colchester

My Space Adventure

I'm going to space in my little rocket ship
To see lots of planets on my big adventurous trip
Starting from Earth, I'm travelling to Mars
To see the red planet, beyond the beautiful stars.
Next is Jupiter, which is orange and white,
As I'm getting closer, it's such a bright light.
Swiftly moving to the golden planet, Saturn,
Wispy rings around it, such a stunning pattern.
My last stop is Uranus,
Which is an amazing pale blue,
It's time to head back to Earth,
I'm coming home to you.

Archie Boorman (9)
Queen Boudica Primary School, Colchester

The InBESTtigators

My favourite show is The InBESTigators,
First up is the creator,
Ezra Banks is the one to thank,
Because he put them all together.
Next is the brains of it all,
Because Maudi Miller is so cool,
She solves every case
As quick as a flash,
So she gets all the cash.
Then there is Kyle Klingson,
He's not good at solving missions,
But he is good at playing football.
Last of all there's Ava,
She's kind and funny
And loves days that are super sunny.

Hannah Radford (9)
Queen Boudica Primary School, Colchester

Space Planets

S pace is tranquil.
P ancake Galaxy is still being discovered.
A rduous journeys await.
C ount the numerous, glittery stars.
E xtraordinary things happen.

P lanets are psychedelic.
L ight years away.
A stronomy helps us learn about intergalactic space.
N eptune with its faded rings.
E xploration missions.
T elescopes help us see outlying galaxies.
S upernova explosions.

Joshuah Gibbons (10)
Queen Boudica Primary School, Colchester

The Planets

Mercury is the hottest of all.
Venus is the second smallest ball.
Earth is where we live but I would rather live on Mars instead.
Mars has millions of hills and is apparently red.
Jupiter is the biggest planet but is not the planet that has a loop.
Saturn has a ring like a hula hoop.
Uranus has a ring that is made out of dust and things.
Neptune is the coldest, I call it the Ice King.
The planets are in a galaxy.
The galaxy is held together by gravity.

Olivia Cawdery (9)
Queen Boudica Primary School, Colchester

Space Is Just Space

U nbelievably beautiful night sky.
N ever know how high.
I deal galaxy that's just so perfect.
V arious planets, each one just so amazing in their own way.
E xcellent solar system keeping people wondering.
R adiant colours that fill my head.
S pectacular stars so bright yet so far.
E cstatic minds that could well blow.

Olivia Bingle (9)
Queen Boudica Primary School, Colchester

A Cow On The Moon

The cow on the moon is big and round.
The moon is vibrant, amazing with ice rings like Saturn.
Even the moon jungles are exquisite to look at
But the crocs are deadly.
The cow is a friendly chum to some
But to others he's no fun.
When day turned to night and the cow got a fright,
He realised it was only a lunar eclipse.

Holly Clynick (9)
Queen Boudica Primary School, Colchester

Rap King

Yo, I'm excellent at rapping,
It's so familiar to me,
Even the government want to see me,
But I'm not sure about over-forties.
It's all over the world,
All over the news,
It's every day, every night,
Like a bit of chicken
And a bit of spice.

Tyler Thompson (10)
Queen Boudica Primary School, Colchester

Illumination

S tars amongst us, may end up in dreams,
T rillions to count, though many are unseen,
A million points of silver light,
R avishing, as they shine so bright,
S ome people may hope to see, the illumination in front of me!

Dylan Secreto (10)
Queen Boudica Primary School, Colchester

The Unidentified Universe

U nidentified Uranus.
N atural Neptune.
I nternational illustration.
V iolent vanguard.
E xpanded Earth.
R uthless rides.
S cientific satellite.
E ligible England.

Ryan Hammett (10)
Queen Boudica Primary School, Colchester

Max

My dog is not a pug
And his name is Max.
He likes sleeping on his rug
With all his snacks.
He rumbles through the park
And chews on my socks.
His fluffy fur is dark,
I love him 'cause he rocks!

Dominik Panek (9)
Queen Boudica Primary School, Colchester

The Moon And The Sun

Stars twinkle everywhere
As the moon comes up and gives a glare.
Then the sun comes up and shines the light,
What a sight.
It brings together family and friends
With joy and love that never ends.

Mia Warr (10)
Queen Boudica Primary School, Colchester

Space Waste

Look around space
There's so much plastic waste
Let's clean up this place
It's so fantastic in space.

Rococo-Rose Theobald (9)
Queen Boudica Primary School, Colchester

Space

Space
Tranquil, incalculable
Levitating, gyrating, orbiting
Filled with perplexing mysteries
Supernovas.

Ty Awoyinfa (9)
Queen Boudica Primary School, Colchester

A Visit To The Solar System

One day I went to visit the stars
But then I saw a volcano erupting from Planet Mars.
I know it must be the biggest one there
But when I saw the eruption I shot up with a scare.
And it was then when I saw the sun
It looked like a pool of glimmering fun.
That was when I had to explore more,
But all I saw was darkness which meant a bore.
Saturn has some old broken wings,
We're not sure if Jupiter even has these things.
The place where us human beings live is called Earth.
That will show you how much it is worth.
The one with the raging storm is Jupiter.
The size of this planet might make feel better
The one closest to the sun is Mercury.
It can reach 427° but can cool down easily,
The one with tremendous winds is Neptune,
When you visit it you meet your doom.

The hottest planet in the solar system is Venus.
The heat it contains is furious.
The last planet to talk about is Uranus
But most just say that it is mysterious!

Abhimanyu Kirubaharan (7)
Rosedale Primary School, Hayes

Koalas

Koalas are cute...
I see them all the time,
In the trees and up high in the sky, though
that part is only in my dream.
Whenever I see them, I beam, I beam
I beam all the time.
In my dreams I see them fall from the sky like
diamonds.
Oh they look so brown and bright.
Koalas, koalas, oh koalas, they're so cute.
They're so cute but the baby ones...
They look so sweet, beautiful and strong.
So fluffy and fuzzy,
It's not hard to say they're cute
especially when they hang from the trees,
But I just love them there.
The big and the little ones.
When I see them in the trees they look like spiral
koala falling
Koalas are so cute,
It was remarkable and incredible to see them at
the zoo.

They look as soft as a snowflake.
I have one at home but it's just a toy,
My cuddly, cuddly toy and friend.
I hope they're okay after the bushfires in Australia.

Ruth Marsh (7)
Rosedale Primary School, Hayes

Imaginary Friends

I sit down and I close my eyes,
I forget all my worries and cries,
And create an imaginary world in my mind.
Then I see a silver bunny leaving a trail of magic behind.
Now I see a clear fox coming out of the shadows.
The lovely fox spots the bunny and chases her in the magical meadows.
Now, out gallops a golden stallion, galloping on air,
He stops and swishes his incredible hair.
Out steps a shy deer with a chestnut coat,
And as she takes tiny steps, she starts to float.
The bunny and fox stop chasing,
The young stallion stops racing,
And the young deer with a chestnut coat
Stops and all the animals gently start to float.
It's fun when you have imaginary friends,
But it's time for this fun to end.

Emilia Liepsch (8)
Rosedale Primary School, Hayes

The Fastest Land Animal!

Cheetahs are the best,
You can put them to the test.
To communicate, they chirp,
They never roar.
They can be bored.
They crouch across the African savannah,
In that sneaky, creeping manner.
For them hunting is as easy as pie,
As they speed across the land willing things to die.
Gazelles are fast food for cheetahs,
At 110kph they always manage to catch their feeders.
Cheetah cubs can camouflage,
Just like a chameleon entourage.
They look like honey badgers,
If a lion walks by he will scream like daggers.
And say, "Bye-bye!"
It's time to fly.
Mighty cheetahs! Mighty creatures!

Amir Gianni Cole (8)
Rosedale Primary School, Hayes

A Superhero's Day

Big, black bombs are ticking!
Fingers are clicking,
In the sky, there I sway,
Don't worry, I'm here to save the day!

Roaring, rampaging screams!
Will the sun ever beam?
Thunderous alarms are beeping,
Burglars are shameless, they're sneaking!

Oof! That was a tough, tiring day!
Who's to say?
Life as a superhero is hard,
It's easier to write a million birthday cards!

Too many crimes,
What to do?
I must be there on time,
Well I saved the day (again), phew!

The sun is smiling
And I'm flying.
We're now all happy,
So is Grandpa Pappy!

Zahra Ahmad (9)
Rosedale Primary School, Hayes

Beasts

You and I don't like beasts,
They're usually located in the East.
They are terrible brutes,
Truly they are not cute.
Boom, boom, boom! They're here and there,
Without a doubt they're in your hair.

They're not that good at writing,
But they're great when it comes to biting.
They have giant claws,
Much bigger than a puppy's paws.
They fight you with their tremendous kicks,
Then beat you up with their horrible flicks.

Now you know they're not that nice,
Even worse than a group of mice.

Alesha Seda (9)
Rosedale Primary School, Hayes

The Half-Human And Half-Animal

I want to become an astronaut
And discover new things
I'm in school, actually it's an academy today
We are learning about space.
My dad used to be an astronaut
But he disappeared in January.
When everybody started back
It made me upset.
I met a boy named Andrew,
He was kind and polite.
I felt like I wanted to hop in the next rocket
And ship out to space.
We went to Mars!
It looked glorious and we saw the stars twinkle and shine bright.
Suddenly I heard a swoosh!
Coming towards me it was a half-human, half-animal...

Malachi Tobias (8)
Rosedale Primary School, Hayes

Liverpool

Liverpool is the best team ever
They always aim to win the game
Mané, Salah and Firmino scoring goals
Liverpool relying on Alisson.

Over the years Liverpool have won titles
The FA Cup, Premier League and Champions League
Making fans proud and Klopp smile
While Man United put their fans in denial.

Walking into Anfield, hold your head up high
Fans singing 'You'll Never Walk Alone'
With hope in our hearts and pride in our team.

Top of the Premier League
Liverpool Football Club is the best.

Rahul Bhakri (8)
Rosedale Primary School, Hayes

Sharks Are Deadly

S lithering in the ocean like a snake.
H ungry mouth zooming through the ocean.
A fter meals of the day
R esting very heavily.
K ing-sized animal coming through.
S nap!

"**A** rgh!"
R un for your life.
E veryone is going to be dead.

D ivers better watch out
E specially for the great white.
A re they going to be safe?
D ash through the ocean.
L ike a blazing fast cheetah underwater.
Y es, now it is safe.

Mihir Lohani (8)
Rosedale Primary School, Hayes

The Beast Of The Seas

T he massive ship roamed the deep ocean.
I n the Atlantic it eventually started to sink...
Splash!
T he people better leave the ship.
A s everyone jumped in the water, the Titanic halved.
"**N** ooo!" screamed Captain Smith.
I know it fell to a watery grave.
C ould it fall like rain to its death?

S inking slowly, shaking and shivering.
A nd it was ripped open.
N ever had anyone seen such a tragedy.
K icking the sand away, the Titanic rotted.

Reece Hogan-Marks (8)
Rosedale Primary School, Hayes

Titanic

It was big and large.
It even had a garage.
It was very white with black and blue
But now it's not very new.
The captain was very mean
But he was very clean.

One bright beautiful night
Some people took fright
As they were going on a journey
But they were going on it firmly.
There were big thunderstorms
And the engine was not the norm.

All of a sudden with a big crash
Into an iceberg, with a big bash.
They fell into the water step by step
As the story of the Titanic is still kept.

Yusuf Rustamkhail (9)
Rosedale Primary School, Hayes

Kittens

Us kittens are cute and I purr all day.
I may be fluffy and white and my eyes are light blue.
Meow, meow!
I am cute, I love sleeping because it's relaxing.
I love my mum and I drink her milk, as white as fog.
Hope you know Mummy, I love you!
Meow, meow, meow! Ha ha!
My eyes inside are as light as the sky.
I hate salty water 'cause my white fur is as white as snow.
I hate frost but I'm gonna get used to it.
I love being a kitten, I'm so furry,
But sometimes I'm shy.

Lois Trim (7)
Rosedale Primary School, Hayes

Unicorn Night

U nicorn, unicorn, you are so bright.
N ight night, sleep so right.
I cannot believe you came true my dear unicorn.
C ome, come I will make you shine.
O h glow so bright like a golden light.
R un, run, catch like, I'm spying on you.
N ight night, don't be harmed.

N o, I will save you.
I can't believe you're with me.
G o, so they don't break your heart
H a ha run away or die.
T o the underworld.

Mehreen Menaal (8)
Rosedale Primary School, Hayes

Under The Sea

U nder the sea,
N ew things to see.
D o you want to see creatures under the sea?
E ven if you do now let's go recap under the sea...
R ecap! Come on! Let's go under the sea.

T he sea! Oh wow! Are you looking at the starfish?
H ey! Are you having fun in the ocean?
E ww! Look at that slimy octopus in the deep.

S ee now what we learn! It is fun in a marine land.
E ww! Look, seaweed!
A rgh! A shark with sharp teeth.

Mominah Mohammed (7)
Rosedale Primary School, Hayes

In Space

The stars are as white as snowflakes.
The red rocket ship is as red as fire
And the stars are as shiny as glitter.
The Earth is as blue as the blue sky
But the moon looks like white round cheese.
The rocketship sounds like fire.
The dark sky in space is a beautiful galaxy colour.
The rocketship is as fast as a motorbike.
An astronaut is as brave as a knight
And the moon is as white as white snow.
The moon is as hard as a rock
But the stars are as white as white snow and white clouds.

Louisa-Jayne Farr (7)
Rosedale Primary School, Hayes

Under The Sea

U rchins have spikes like a capital X.
N emo fish swim with fast fins flying.
D eep in the sea whales live. It is a big ball!
E merald comes in beautiful shapes.
R oom inside like a cake.

T he jellyfish sting with their colourful stripes.
H ere's an octopus which is sad.
E ach one of them is extremely beautiful every day...

S quid show their black smoke.
E very day something happens.
A ny colourful way.

Tolunimi Shodipe (8)
Rosedale Primary School, Hayes

Spring Is Here

Finally, spring is here
It's the lovely time of year
Leaves are green
What a beautiful scene
Flowers smile at me
There goes a happy bee
What would we do if this season wasn't created?
We'd be forever frustrated!

Finally, spring is here
It's the most lovely time of year
Birds high up in the trees
And children with lots of ease.

Finally, spring is here
It's the most lovely time of year.

Ethan Jacob Dalrymple (8)
Rosedale Primary School, Hayes

Under The Ocean

U rchins are spiky and friendly.
N ever touch angry sharks.
D ark oceans are deep and dangerous.
E els are grey and funny.
R ed octopuses are dreadful.

T urtles are the best.
H armful jellyfish sting.
E merald stones hidden in the coral are precious!

S tarfish are naughty and colourful.
E vil people catch all types of fish.
A wful anemones are slimy.

Jiya Kaul (8)
Rosedale Primary School, Hayes

Summer

Oh summer, summer, that's my season.
It's like spring,
But the sea is as warm as it can be.
I play all day.
The sun is a big ball of air.
It's like you watch flowers grow with some heat,
It's so sweet.
I love the sun with all my heart.
I wouldn't leave in a cart.
You're as pretty as can be,
Sitting in the sun.
Oh no, it's past 8 o'clock.
Bye-bye my sweet sun,
Go and have some fun.

Shania Jhem (8)
Rosedale Primary School, Hayes

Animals

The cat is stripy.
The cat is as serious as a cat boss.
The cat is cute as she is asking for food.
Cute green eyes.
Funny as a puffy dog.
Little as a fish.
Thick little whiskers.
Small, little ears.
Hairy, biteable, adorable cat.
Loveable, happy, scratchy cat.
Moody, little, pokey nose.
Sharp little teeth.
Cuddly as a pillow.
Grey as the ground.
Big as a bear.
Hairy as a gorilla.
I love my cat.

Hibhah Malik (8)
Rosedale Primary School, Hayes

My Favourite Thing Is Santa Claus

S anta Claus is magical
A nd with his reindeer, he won't fall.
N o one can make a miracle except him.
T oys are getting delivered,
A lready for Christmas Day.

C hildren wake up,
L ook what I see.
A big pile of toys just for me.
U mbrellas, yes! Just what I wanted.
S ugar I love, sweets I love too. Every December,
Christmas Day is waiting just for you.

Freya Wyle (8)
Rosedale Primary School, Hayes

My Favourite Thing

M inecraft has emerald grass and deep mines.
I n Minecraft you will find diamonds.
N o monsters in the Cave of Dark.
E at shiny gold apples to get extra lives.
C rafting jewellery on Minecraft is very hard.
R ats are the worst creatures on Minecraft.
A t Minecraft you will find gold.
F ind gems in mines to make beautiful things.
T o mine diamonds you need an iron pickaxe.

Daniel Valys (8)
Rosedale Primary School, Hayes

Winter

Beautiful crystals come down from the sky
And ice is on the floor, so I can glide.
Snowballs everywhere.
It is very cold, freezing cold.
It is snowy.
It is dark too.
That's when I want to go to the park.

It's warm inside.
That's why I want a mug.
A mug of hot cocoa.

Weather is chilly.
I am cold.
The sun sets quickly.
Things get tricky.
All because of the ice.

Iyla Dhaliwal (9)
Rosedale Primary School, Hayes

All About My Family

Family is the best ever!
Have the greatest father in the world.
My mom is lovely...
It's fun playing with my family,
Love my family always.

F amily is as strong as a knight
A nd I have the best father.
M y mom looks beautiful, like a princess.
I t's fun playing football with my brother.
L ove my family always.
Y ou're the best family that anyone has.

Prabhnoor Arora (7)
Rosedale Primary School, Hayes

Haunted House

H aunted house of doom,
A pproximately noon.
U sually you'll find ghosts creeping around,
N ever good, always bad,
T he night is the worst time,
E very day, death,
D on't ever come here.

H ow creepy,
O uch, ouch, blood!
U sually death,
S ometimes you'll regret this,
E very night children disappear.

Ria Bal Bhakri (8)
Rosedale Primary School, Hayes

Monsters

Monsters are scary and stinky,
They can eat you.
They are hairy.
They have stinky breath.
They have sharp fangs.
They have one eye or two.
They can eat yummy humans.
They are immense creatures,
They can live in your house or in caves.
They are wild,
They will chase you in the woods.
They are really ugly.
Sometimes they fight other monsters.
They are very dreadful.

Petros Sampo (7)
Rosedale Primary School, Hayes

Aliens In Outer Space Today

Aliens are silly billy space animals
That live with the English talking stars
Which are in outer space
Where space rockets like to race.
The planets, even the Earth, are tiny balls
That bounce on a wall.
Bounce, bounce, bounce!
"Stop! There's a runaway star!"
On a small bar
Which is like a shiny globe that is zooming away.
Oh, have a good outer space day!

Muskan Patel (8)
Rosedale Primary School, Hayes

Ssss... Snakes!

Long, short, thin and fat.
Slithering around, without making a sound!
People can be scared of me,
But treat me well and there's nothing to fear about me.
Even when I'm big you can easily treat me like a pet.
Whenever you want to have a pet snake like me.
Sometimes I bite, sometimes I poison.
Some people are scared, some people are not
And some want a pet like me!

Elizabeth Allen (8)
Rosedale Primary School, Hayes

The Ocean

Tiptoe into the ocean,
A wonderful sight.
Dazzling blues,
Worldwide!

The waves approach, *splash!*
They cover your eyes,
Sea creatures swim with different colours,
As cold as the Atlantic.

A steady flow to the ocean's waves,
Orange and yellow reflection when the sunsets,
The rain builds it up,
Overflowing the cold, chilly air!

Mia Louise Curl (8)
Rosedale Primary School, Hayes

The Sea

The sea is blue like the light sky.
The sea has fish under the water.
The sea is watery like the jellyfish.
The rain has water like the ocean.
The fish swim, swim, swim.
The water is all around the world.
The jellyfish is as wobbly as a jelly.
The fish swim fast, fast, fast.
The fish are colourful like the rainbow.
And the sun is shining as bright as a mirror.

Leticia Venturini (7)
Rosedale Primary School, Hayes

Magic Box

M agic boxes are special.
A little star comes out like a flash of light.
G reat rainbow strings pop out!
I look inside and there are red and orange sweets.
C ome out sweets! Pop like a rainbow.

B ig star, do you have a face?
O h my goodness, golden-coloured confetti!
X mas-coloured strings are coming out.

Maryam Shugaa (7)
Rosedale Primary School, Hayes

Under The Sea

A gorgeous blue fish swimming in the sea.
A colourful coral sat in front of me.
The ocean, as blue as the sky,
The fish, as bright as the sun up high.

Starfish are spiky and rainbow-coloured.
Sharks are scary but friendly though.
You can see dolphins swimming at the edge of the Earth.

Did you know, whales are the biggest mammals on Earth?

Haram Qazi (8)
Rosedale Primary School, Hayes

The Titanic

T he Titanic was massive.
I t hit an iceberg in the freezing Atlantic Ocean, kaboom!
T he Titanic broke down.
A s fast as possible, to the bottom of the sea it sank.
"**N** ooo!" yelled the captain. "We are sinking!"
I t was the end of the Titanic.
C ould some people still be alive?

Chinedu Okam (9)
Rosedale Primary School, Hayes

Giggling Glamorous Galaxy

Giggling glamorous galaxy
Out of this world!
The stars are shining sparkly
The dew of the galaxy stars are out of this world.
The stars are abominable and outrageous.
Oh yeah!
The beautiful bouncy blue glitter bounces off stars...
Falling off our heads and glistening.
Goodbye giggling, glamorous galaxy
It's morning now!

Toludari Shodipe (8)
Rosedale Primary School, Hayes

Outer Space

Wonderful space, lots to explore.
Now imagine space junk floating just like a shark.

The moon is shining just like a bright light.
Shining in your eyes with all its might.
Planets like Pluto, Jupiter and Mars,
The Milky Way and billions of stars.

Rockets, spaceships, UFOs,
Mean, ugly creatures with thirty-six toes.

Millan Dhaliwal (7)
Rosedale Primary School, Hayes

My Family

F amily is fun! I love my family.
A ll the characters can make a big happy family.
M y mum is lovely and all my family.
I t's fun playing tennis and I'm Dennis.
L ove my friends, they are enjoyable to be with.
Y es, I'm big but my family is bigger.

Dennis Radu (8)
Rosedale Primary School, Hayes

Best Friends Forever

Me and my friends are forever,
Even when we are not together.
Sometimes I look up to the sky
And think what it would be like to fly.
If I could go over the moon
I would take my best friends too.

To have a great friend,
Till the end; best friends forever.

Lily Katie Saunders (8)
Rosedale Primary School, Hayes

In The Snow

In the snow...
The breeze is cold
The polar bears roam
The white trees grow
Then the footprints go
The snow melts
The white trees go
Polar bears go
The breeze is warm
The birds sing
The bears come out
The fish swim
The rabbits run.

Alfie Salmon (8)
Rosedale Primary School, Hayes

Candy

Candy is sweet,
Better than a musical beat.
Lollies are yummy,
Better than a gummy.
Candy is a treat,
So sweet.
Sour Patch Kids are sour,
Just like a superpower.
I love candy,
Better than anything.
Candy!

Alvin Chagwedere (9)
Rosedale Primary School, Hayes

All About Dogs

A dog likes to scare cats.
Dogs can run really fast.
A dog will protect his owner and fight for him
If he knows the outcome.
If you have a guard dog
It will protect you no matter what.
A dog has brown and black skin.

Makel Hewitt (8)
Rosedale Primary School, Hayes

Outer Space

S pace doesn't have oxygen.
P lanets are very humongous.
A stronauts need lots of oxygen to stay in space.
C hildren are too young to go into space.
E dges of the universe are not discovered.

Ahmed Shahid (7)
Rosedale Primary School, Hayes

Space

Space is as black as darkness.
In space the sun is as bright as shiny metal.
In space there is no oxygen.

Space is as cold as winter.
Space is full of stars, galaxies and planets.
Space can kill you fast.

Rayan Sahari (7)
Rosedale Primary School, Hayes

Out Of Space

S pace is where lots of planets are.
P eace and quiet is in space.
A t space there is a planet called Saturn.
C an't people go on Jupiter?
E veryone can't live on Mars.

Niroshan Mathanatheepan (8)
Rosedale Primary School, Hayes

Water And Snow

(A diamante poem)

Water
Clear, still
Splashing, flowing, spilling
Keeps you hydrated, makes you feel cold
Melting, falling, spreading
Glamorous, white
Snow.

Hajrah Bibi (9)
Rosedale Primary School, Hayes

Bobble And Bauble

Once there was a dog called Bobble,
Also a llama called Bauble,
They go in a rocket and zoom off to space,
They can't wait to go to a new place,
When they get there they meet an alien,
Slimy and gross, he likes Italian,
Bobble and Bauble get taken,
So they are shaken,
They soon make friends,
So the alien ends,
So now Bobble and Bauble are back to Earth.

Ellie Emily Stretton (10)
Ryecroft CE Middle School, Rocester

Mars

Mars looks as nice as chocolate bars,
It's as red as a car,
Very fierce and loud,
It can sometimes be as loud as a storm cloud,
It's very round and red,
It should be called Fred,
Mars is the best,
Now I am going to rest.

Bethany Palmer (10)
Ryecroft CE Middle School, Rocester

Love Letter

A love letter is luscious
Especially when it's unexpected
Two people, blue-eyed and beautiful
In love at high school
Sending notes to each other
Feeling special, secretive and sassy
Love is all around
It has no bounds.

Felicity Johnson (10)
Ryecroft CE Middle School, Rocester

Monster

He is as tall as a mountain
He is as strong as a hundred men
He is faster than ten cheetahs
His roar is as loud as twenty lightning storms
He lives on Planet Bear Heart
He can kill anything in his path
That is all I know.

Harrison Rai (9)
Ryecroft CE Middle School, Rocester

Colours

Orange is a pumpkin,
Yellow is a lemon,
Green is a clover,
And brown is a bear eating a melon,
Purple is blossom,
Blue is the sea,
Black is night,
And red is a cherry.

Freya Whomersley (10)
Ryecroft CE Middle School, Rocester

Football

Players
Fast, fit
Dribble, kick, strike
Sportsmanship, players on a field
Bouncy, controlled strike
Round, spotty
Ball.

Jamie Barr (10)
Ryecroft CE Middle School, Rocester

Earth And Mars

Earth
Colourful, beautiful
Zoom, bounce, red ball of stone,
Rotate, roll, spin
Red, small
Mars.

Hollie-Mai Laidler (10)
Ryecroft CE Middle School, Rocester

Out Of This World

Our world is dying
And people are crying.
If we could stop smoking
Then people would stop choking,
That would be out of this world.

Our world is dying
And people are crying
If we could stop bushfires,
Then we could stop political liars,
That would be out of this world.

Our world is dying
And people are crying.
If we could stop climate change
Then we could stop hunters killing a wide range,
That would be out of this world.

Our world is dying
And people are crying.
If we could keep our sea sapphire-blue
Then the world would be better for you and me,
That would be out of this world.

Our world is dying
And people are crying.
If we could keep our grass emerald green
Then we could have no smoke and things could be seen,
That would be out of this world.

Annabel Brogan (9)
Smarden Primary School, Smarden

Out Of This World

O ut of this world animals are dying.
U se your life to save animals.
T op up care for animals.

O f all the animals choose all of them.
F rom all the animals we love you.

T o top off, how would you like to be an animal dying?
H ow would you feel, it is not nice!
I s this how you want the world to be?
S eas are getting higher, help us!

W ould you like to buy an animal?
O r animals that you like.
R yan likes animals, he cares.
L ook, look, look, animals are dying because of us.
D o you care about animals?

Maisie Bottle (8)
Smarden Primary School, Smarden

My Seaside

I like to look at...
Shiny, slimy starfish shining in the sea like a piece of jewellery.
Salty sandcastles on the beach like some Play-Doh.
Flipping fish furiously doing tricks in the sea.

I like the smell of...
Frosty, floppy fish falling off the plate like you have just turned eight.
Icy ice cream quickly slipping off the crusty cone.
Smoky sausages on the barbecue like a hot chicken.

I like to touch...
Slimy seaweed slipping out of my hand in the sea.
Tasty towels drying me like a hairdryer.
Slippery sand quickly falling out my hand.

I like to hear...
Seagulls screaming in the sky.
Junkyard jet skis cruising on top of the water like a speedboat.
Waves crashing down on the water like a storm.

Jenson Henney (8)
St Clare's Catholic Primary School, Coalville

My Seaside

I like to look at...
The big blue sea like the sky high up above us.
The seagulls squawking so loud, like a horn hooting.
The big yellow sun rising in the east and setting down in the west.
A sandcastle getting sucked into the sea by the waves.

I like to smell...
The barbecue smoke through the air, making me slobber.
I like the smell of the blue, salty sea sucking castles one by one.
Hot dogs smelling tastier than ever.
The suncream smoothing down on people.

I like to touch...
The cold sea especially when it's cold.
I play with my sand bucket by touching them to build.
I touch the yellow dusty sand that is lying on the ground.

I like to hear...
The jet skis skidding across the water smoothly.
I like to hear dolphins jumping and landing with a splash.
The loud music beat bringing the sand up and down.
I like to hear the crabs clicking their fingers.

Joshua Chandy (8)
St Clare's Catholic Primary School, Coalville

My Seaside

I like to look at...
Boats bobbing in the waves like a ball bouncing.
Seaweed shaking slowly on the seashore.
Parasols protecting people like a hat blocking the sun from our heads.

I like to listen to...
Seagulls cheeping, croaking like a bad as a bullfrog's song.
Waves waving and whacking the shore loudly like an elephant hitting the ground.
Music beating loudly like a party all gone wrong.

I like the smell of...
Coconuts, as creamy as a sundae in a microwave.
Barbecue in a grill, glazing gorgeously, attracting seagulls like a magnet connecting to metal.
Fish flying frantically trying to escape a shark, like a human in a jungle trying to escape a tiger.

I like to touch...
Anemones closing in my hand, cosily like a baby in a crib.
Twigs touching under the might of an elephant trying to squash it.
Sand being squeezed on the floor like a slug being trod on.

Isaac Reed (8)
St Clare's Catholic Primary School, Coalville

My Seaside

I like to look at...
The people splashing in the sea after a nice relax on the sand.
The tall palm tree blowing in the wind.
The extremely bright blue sky with seagulls flying by.

I like to smell...
Lots of people licking ice cream bought from the local shop.
The beach basketball team throwing the ball into the sky.
Fish swimming in the salty sea like ants in a formicarium.

I like to touch...
Quickly heated hot rocks shining like diamonds in the sun.
People crabbing at the crabbing docks with lines as long as snakes.
Sand as soft as snow glistening in the flaming sun.

I like to hear...
Rough waves toppling over surfers who swiftly slide on the waves.
Voices echoing in the waves as if someone said the same thing over and over again.
Whales singing as loudly as a boombox on full volume.

Sam Smith (8)
St Clare's Catholic Primary School, Coalville

My Seaside

I like to look at ...
The sea swishing like a wishing well in the sunlight.
The seagulls flying as high as the sun rising.
The dolphin dropping his tail in the glimmery sea.

I like the smell of...
Sun cream going on your skin like the sun going through your body.
Barbecues and the scrumptious smell of fish and chips.

I like the touch of...
The yellow spade and bucket going through the sand.
The seaweed in the sea, sinking like a submarine with no fuel.
Towels wet in the sea.

I like to hear...
Babies crying like a siren when the waves come near.
Chatting like there is no tomorrow on the beach.
Waves coming like something is coming in the sea.

Tanya Ncube (7)
St Clare's Catholic Primary School, Coalville

My Seaside

I like to look at...
The parasols prancing along the wind like a happy couple.
The waves wailing in the breeze.
The seagulls squawking like a squirrel.

I like the smell of...
Sweets, scrumptious ice cream in a cone.
The crackling sound coming from the delicious sand.
The suncream smells like it's burning on my face.

I like to touch...
The bucket and spade burning with the children.
Seaweed, green as grass like a grasshopper.
Towels as dry as the sand.

I like to hear...
Whales singing to each other like an audition.
The disco beat wanting people to dance with the dolphin jumping in the sky just like a butterfly.

Charlotte Chadwick (8)
St Clare's Catholic Primary School, Coalville

My Seaside

I like to look at...
The jet skis cruising on the blue sea at my seaside.
Blue sea big and very wet water to have fun.
Sandcastles slowly being built on the sand.

I like the smell of...
Ice cream swirled on a cone as delicious as a bit of chocolate.
A barbecue on the sand, flaming hot like a bottle of hot sauce.

I like to hear...
A whale's song, beautiful and calm.
Ocean waves going up and down like a big hill.
People chatting as loud as a jungle.

I like to touch...
Hot rocks on the floor, as hot as a desert.
Sand in the sun, easy to break.
Goggles to swim in the big blue sea, having fun.

Raphael Fowkes (8)
St Clare's Catholic Primary School, Coalville

My Seaside

I like to touch...
A soft, fluffy towel after I've been in the cold water.
A smooth, colourful coral reef.
Soft, silky sand running through my hands.

I like to smell...
Ice cream melting like a cube of ice.
A hot barbecue on a sunny day.
Fish and chips burning like a flame.

I like to look at...
A seahorse swimming in cold water.
A dolphin suddenly splashing around.
Children building sandcastles like a master.

I like to listen to...
Dolphins splashing and jumping like a Bianca in cold water.
Ocean waves whacking the shore.
A whale song humming like a bird.

Bianca Neagu (7)
St Clare's Catholic Primary School, Coalville

My Seaside

I like to look at...
The blue sea when I go to the beach.
Boats on the sea, sailing away across the water.
Sandcastles on the sand with seashells for decorations.

I like to smell...
The salty sea.
The barbecue roasting chicken.
The suncream's smell on the owner's lap.

I like the touch of...
Seaweed, slimy and slithery, green as a pear.
Buckets and spades made out of plastic like a plastic bottle.
Sand slowly coming out of my hands.

I like to listen to...
People chatting loudly.
The waves quickly collapsing.
The cars passing by with gas coming out.

Felicia Ruwodo (8)
St Clare's Catholic Primary School, Coalville

My Seaside

I like to look...
At playful seahorses playing in the water.
Sandcastles being built by people.
Waves on the sea splashing and roaring like a lion.

I like to smell...
The salty sea with sea creatures in it.
Ice cream in a cone flavoured strawberry.
Suncream being rubbed on the people on the beach.

I like to touch...
The yellow, soft sand on the beach.
Balls rolling past the sea.
Water swishing past me.

I like to hear...
The music being played by singers.
Waves on the sea crashing down.
Dolphins splashing in the water like a car in a race.

Lacey-May Wilson (7)
St Clare's Catholic Primary School, Coalville

My Seaside

I like to look at...
A dolphin that is as blue as the sky.
A seagull as white as a plover.
A dolphin as blue as the water.

I like to smell...
I can smell sizzling fish and chips.
I can smell the hot barbecues.
I can smell the cold ice cream.

I like to touch...
I like to play in the sand.
I like to play with a bucket and spade.
I like to lie on the towel.

I like to listen to the seagulls.
I like to listen to the dolphins.
I like to listen to the whales.

Ellie Posnett (7)
St Clare's Catholic Primary School, Coalville

My Seaside

I like to look at...
The white clouds in the sky, they are like cotton wool.

I like to smell...
Fresh fish and chips in the sea air.

I like to touch...
The freezing cold water.

I like to hear...
The sharks splashing in the sea.

I like to look at...
The flouncing seagulls in the morning, flying in the beautiful sky.

I like to smell...
The smooth Slushies when people eat drinking them.

I like to touch...
The silky hot sand.

Tyler Walker (7)
St Clare's Catholic Primary School, Coalville

My Seaside

I like to look at...
Bright boats in the sea fishing for food.
Sandcastles with pearly shells on the top, sparkling like diamonds.
People skimming rocks in the beautiful sea.
Beautiful dolphins in the sea, jumping up and down.

I like to touch...
Patterned seashells washed up on the beach.
Slippery sand going through my rough hands into the sea.
Delicious ice cream, as cold as a freezer.

Noel Cassidy (8)
St Clare's Catholic Primary School, Coalville

Light Years

As I travel through time to a faraway place
I pack my bags and tie my shoelace
I look at my watch as an hour passes by
I jump in my rocket and get ready to fly
I can't cut my hair or bend my legs
I can't hang my ripped clothes up with broken pegs
Can't scream goodbye or run away
And all these years I've wondered why my hair is turning grey
And my eyes are turning black
Darkness running through my body, I cannot give it back
I'm withering away as the time flies past
I'm worried this journey may be my last.

Jessica Flynn (10)
St Edward's Royal Free Ecumenical Middle School, Windsor

Who Is Your Hero?

Who is your hero?
Are they powerful?
Are they cunning?
Did they save people?

Maybe they're from DC or Marvel,
Is it a big bulk,
The Incredible Hulk?
Or maybe he's too good to buy,
An indestructible Hawkeye?

Is he a footballer?
The football besty,
Lionel Messi?
Maybe a manager too good to swap,
Funny and crucial Jürgen Klopp.

Are they from the Royal family?
Meghan he has begun to marry,
The important Prince Harry,
Known by a billion,
An amazing Prince William.

Or is it a villain,
Who walks around at night,
Giving everyone a fright,
Who is called Dracula?
Or a man with cards from poker,
The terrifying Joker?

Could it be an author?
She makes people go wowing
That is JK Rowling
There might be a good author for you
Called Dr Seuss.

Aidan Gallagher (9)
St Edward's Royal Free Ecumenical Middle School, Windsor

A Midnight Chase

A fox,
A fox, quiet and still
Innocent it is not
Waiting patiently
For its feeding slot.

Playful shall it seem
Satisfaction must be achieved
Something appetising is rustling
Through these thin strands of grass.

As quiet as a mouse
Scurrying through a silent house
The fox gets ready, waiting
For its pounce.

Boing!
There goes the fox
With his soft furry paws
Longing to place its prey in its jaws.

"Run! Run! Make it a habit
You can't catch me, I'm a little grey rabbit!"

The rabbit made a miraculous escape
Making it out with only one or two scrapes
And that was the end of the fox's meal (so it seemed)
Still his appetite must be relieved.

Logan Allen (11)
St Edward's Royal Free Ecumenical Middle School, Windsor

New Kid In Town

There's a new kid in my town
I don't know what to do.
Shall I introduce myself?
Or leave her all alone?
She's a shy little girl
Who's now in my class,
Her name is little Lucy
And she's very good at art.
She's a very smart girl;
Smarter than an adult.
She's a very smiley girl, indeed
And I like her little bow.
When I walk around
I never say hello,
I really want to be friends with her
But I can't pluck up the courage to.
Maybe I just say hi to her to get me started up...

Florence Griffiths (10) & Grace Fowler (10)
St Edward's Royal Free Ecumenical Middle School, Windsor

The Seasons Sing

I love the seasons, so warm, so cold,
They never seem to get that old.
When the rain falls to the summer's heat,
I love walking on the beach with my bare feet.
I watch the sea level rise and I feel I've been taken up to the sky.
I know that I'm on a bright and upbeat ride through the spring field, here I glide.
Red, golden-yellow autumn leaves fall and as they touch the ground the leaves curl up in a ball.
The range of snow, sun, wind and rain, I never want the seasons to change.

Sophia Comitti (9)
St Edward's Royal Free Ecumenical Middle School, Windsor

Our Chance

The wind blows in the willows
With a huff and a puff
The wind blows in the willows
Blowing away all the stuff

The ice caps are falling
With a stride but no pride
The ice caps are falling
Into the ocean below

The forests are burning
No stop so the world may pop
The forests are burning
No more life on Earth, no new birth

Life is over, it's like someone hit it with a bulldozer
Climate change is here, there's no escape, oh dear.

Finn Eaton (11)
St Edward's Royal Free Ecumenical Middle School, Windsor

My Magical Box

I will put in my box...

An enchanted, mysterious fruit from the tropical forest,
A pearl from the beautiful, blue, transparent sea,
An orange book from the ancient times,
And a pink, pretty, pale rose key.

I will put in my box...

A scale from a fire-breathing dragon,
A bright, broken bulb from the haunted basement,
An orange, red, yellow flame from the bright, eye-blinding sun,
And the fluffiest, funky, fizzy flamingo from Asia.

Luisa Santomo (9)
St Edward's Royal Free Ecumenical Middle School, Windsor

Goal!

When I sink into my pillow
I float into my dream
A world where anything is possible
And that's just for me.

Football is the game I love
It's so thrilling and exciting
I'm the world's best female striker
Running up the pitch like lightning.

It's match day, tension is running high
The teams are on a draw
The crowd chant my name, "Olivia!"
With the winning goal they roar!

Olivia Rutland (10)
St Edward's Royal Free Ecumenical Middle School, Windsor

Under The Sea

U nder the sea it is peaceful
N ear the coral reefs it's colourful
D eep in the sea is where the fish want to be
E verywhere in the coral reefs fish live peacefully
R emarkably deep

T he best part is to swim past a graceful whale
H ow do fish breathe?
E verything is blue

S alty seawater makes a great home for fish
E verything is wet when you're under the sea
A s clear as crystal is what you should expect
when you go under the sea.

Paige Bell (9)
St Hilary's Primary School, St Leonards

Monsters

My fear is black
I can see the violent one-eyed fiend coming near
I can feel the fear tingling down my spine
It tastes like a bitter fruit in my mouth
I can hear the stamps getting closer and closer
I can smell the awful stench of the ogre, it smells like rotten eggs.

Abdulmaleeq Usman (9)
St Hilary's Primary School, St Leonards

Sweet Waffles

W onderful sugary snack
A s good as gold
F antastic, flavourful delight
F resh goodness unfolding in your mouth
L ight to the touch
E ven with Nutella.

Emily Queen (9)
St Hilary's Primary School, St Leonards

Their Lesson Learned

When I was young I met a girl
Who thought she was the best in the world.

All the girls at school laughed at her
While I was shy and tried to speak to her.

She was friendly so I was nice
We both made friends in a trice.

She asked me over and over again
"Why do they laugh at you and me?"

"It's because you're different than most of them
And that's why we have to stick to the rules."

"Why do they do that? There is no point
If it cannot hurt us there is no point."

"It's because they are evil, wicked and mean
It may be hard for you to be seen.

But we'll do our best to not give up
And give those girls a smack in the back.

If we dig deep and finish strong
We'll be out of this school before long."

So together they went and faced the crowd
And afterwards, they felt really quite proud.

Never would they give up again
After all this was their lesson.

Always dig deep and finish strong
You'll be out of your difficulty before long.

Lucy Blatchford (11)
St Michael's School, Burghclere

The Rocky, Ragged Mountain

I see the mountain high as the sky.
I feel almost as if I can fly.

I take a rope and swing with pride.
I feel as big as a bear inside.

I pull myself up the steep and rocky mountain.
I feel like I'm wading through a fountain.

Treacherous, terrible, tall and jagged.
I feel I am a little haggard.

Up to the snow peak I haul myself.
I feel like I'm on top of the world.

Fabian J Kelly (8)
St Michael's School, Burghclere

The Band Of Brothers

The band of brothers
And their names were like others.
Paul, Presley, Daniel, Dick, Frankie and Frenson.
Paul was a hero because he got shot zero.
Presley was friendly and extremely deadly.
Daniel came to harm when he lost an arm.
Dick survived because he was so quick.
Frankie was fast and not afraid of a blast.
Frenson took care of them all.

Joseph Marshall (10)
St Michael's School, Burghclere

Space Knids

Space is a nice place, only when Knids aren't there.
Knids are egg-shaped.
They can turn into any shape they want.
Eating you forever, never ever stopping.
"Come to space," they say.
If you do you'll get chopped up and made into sliced beef.
So if you see one, never scream once,
Because then it will be more than I can say.

Morgan Heath (9)
St Michael's School, Burghclere

Bob The Frog

Bob the frog went to Leicester,
To try and get on a plane.
The bombs were falling, Bob was crawling
And decided to get on a train.

The train got hit and blown to bits,
So Bob got thrown to the floor.
He was hurt along with Bert
And that was the end of the war.

Luke Sudlow (10)
St Michael's School, Burghclere

The Wolf

Silently, silently, in the wood, a wolf prowls.
Deeply and darkly without a sound,
Grabs onto his prey.
Quickly and quietly he goes to his den.
Swiftly, swiftly he runs.
Cleverly but crazily he dodges the guns
Then he trots back to his den.

Amelia Jirgens (10)
St Michael's School, Burghclere

Bad Dreams

Bad dreams, bad dreams,
Worse than bubblegum ice cream,
They are so horrifying that I wake up and I scream
If I have a terrible dream.

Whether it is about a clown or I drown,
I just don't want to have a freaky, terrible dream.

Joseph Malliff (8)
St Michael's School, Burghclere

The Larks

In the sky larks fly through the treetops.
They fly, playing and swooping below the sky.
Happy to be free.
When it snows they quickly fly to a warm country,
When it grows warm they fly back
To enjoy it again and again and again.

Helena Martinez (7)
St Michael's School, Burghclere

Dreams And Nightmares

D reams, dreams.
R ough to romantic.
E nough to scare you but someone nice.
A mazing and outstanding.
M onsters turn dreams into nightmares.
S care you till you scream.

Henry Cullen (8)
St Michael's School, Burghclere

Summit To Shore

As I glided through the breeze,
I heard something trickling below trees.

It was a river, calm and clear,
I thought to myself, *is the ocean near?*

Fluttering through the velvety clouds above,
I glanced into the sunlight and saw a flock of doves.

Gently I gazed around from high to low,
From the snowy peak to the sea below.

I dived down to the silky sandy beach,
The waves came in, it was out of reach.

Beyond the sea the sun was setting,
Horizon azure rose, the moon ascending.

The stars were shining magically bright,
Sparkling like diamonds gleaming in the night.

I hovered over the hill, so gigantic,
The view from the sky was so romantic.

I darted down to the bank at my rest
And I saw my family, they are the best.

My journey has come to an end for it should,
It is time to rest in my little mountain hood.

Gwenan Jones (10)
Ysgol Syr John Rhys, Ponterwyd

Summit To Shore

Dripping slowly from the sky,
I'm a raindrop gliding high.

Reaching down to the mountain,
I see something like a water fountain.

Here I am, in the water source,
I feel the whoosh, it's a mighty force.

I'm stuck in a strong current,
Help! Water everywhere is transparent.

Splash! Smash! Mixing with other water,
I feel a bit of tide water.

Fish swimming in this salty place,
It's like an underwater race.

What's happening now? I'm going up,
I'm rising from this mix-up.

The sun is taking me,
I'm even higher than that tree.

I'm towering up above the sphere,
Where the view is almost clear.

Dripping slowly from the sky,
Again I'm a raindrop gliding high.

Hedd James-Morris (10)
Ysgol Syr John Rhys, Ponterwyd

Summit To Shore

I dived down to the sandy, soft beach
The waves came in, it was out of reach.

I soared in the sky through the clean fresh air
There's something on the beach, it's a funfair.

I was flying, towering in the bright blue sky
I could see other birds fluttering high.

The stunning mountains in the distance were gigantic
The view from up here was romantic.

There were special sea creatures down by the ocean
The tourists were crowding, what a commotion!

Eventually the sun set, the colourful heavens were bright
I hurried to my fluffy bed, it's time to sleep, goodnight.

Ceinwen Davies (8)
Ysgol Syr John Rhys, Ponterwyd

Summit To Shore

S oftly I soared
U p to the heavens, I saw
M assive mountains and
M icroscopic animals beneath my wings.
I was happily soaring, I was happily gliding
T hen a river started flowing down below

T hrough everything in its path
O ver the rocks and all the muddy grass.

S lowly she twisted and turned,
H eavily pouring over the edge
O f the tall mountain.
R oughly the water plunged headfirst into the pond before
E nding its epic journey in the deep blue sea.

Magi Jones (8)
Ysgol Syr John Rhys, Ponterwyd

Why Are You Walking The Snowy Mountain?

Is it a long walk to the top?
You're going to pop!
What is the temperature in the air?
Are you scared of a polar bear?
Do you feel like you can fly?
Are you really, really high?
Who are the people up ahead?
Could your name possibly be Fred?
What mountain are you climbing?
Is it cold?
Is the mountain really, really old?
Did you have a good time on this beautiful mountain climb?

Ryan Griffiths (8)
Ysgol Syr John Rhys, Ponterwyd

YOUNG WRITERS INFORMATION

We hope you have enjoyed reading this book – and that you will continue to in the coming years.

If you're a young writer who enjoys reading and creative writing, or the parent of an enthusiastic poet or story writer, do visit our website **www.youngwriters.co.uk**. Here you will find free competitions, workshops and games, as well as recommended reads, a poetry glossary and our blog. There's lots to keep budding writers motivated to write!

If you would like to order further copies of this book, or any of our other titles, then please give us a call or order via your online account.

Young Writers
Remus House
Coltsfoot Drive
Peterborough
PE2 9BF
(01733) 890066
info@youngwriters.co.uk

Join in the conversation!
Tips, news, giveaways and much more!